Lives and time: a sociological journey

First published in 2002 by the Institute of Education, University of London
20 Bedford Way, London WC1H 0AL

100 years of excellence in education

British Library Cataloguing in Publication Data:
A catalogue record for this publication is available from the British Library

ISBN 0 85473 665 4

Printed in Great Britain by
Peartree Press Limited, Stevenage, Hertfordshire

Typeset by MFK Information Services Limited, Stevenage, Hertfordshire

INSTITUTE OF EDUCATION

University of London

Lives and time: a sociological journey

Julia Brannen

Professor of Sociology of the Family

**Based on a Professorial Lecture
delivered at the Institute of Education,
University of London on 26 June 2002**

Acknowledgements

This lecture has been inspired by many people. I would particularly like to mention Ann Nilsen, without whose influence I may never have turned my attention to time in this lecture. Special thanks are also owed to colleagues with whom I worked on studies drawn upon in the lecture, in particular Peter Moss, Ann Mooney and Suzan Lewis. Thanks also to Emil Brannen.

For organising the occasion of the lecture, I am particularly grateful to the Director, Geoff Whitty; to Elaine Peck and Cathy Bird in the Conference Office; to Tamara Boake, Cathy Shaw and Jethro Perkins in Thomas Coram Research Unit; and to Helen Green in the Press Office. Thanks also to the editorial and marketing team in the Publications Office.

Professor Julia Brannen

Lives and time: a sociological journey

To understand the relationship between lives and time we may begin by turning to poets and storytellers. Some poets have portrayed life as a journey. In the play *The Prince of Homburg*, von Kleist traces life's journey through the growth cycle of trees and shrubs:

> This Life, says the poet, is a journey,
>
> And a short one. Really! From six feet up
>
> Above the earth, down to six feet under.
>
> (Heidrich von Kleist, 1811)

The anonymous poet of 'The Lament of the Old Woman of Beare' also describes the journey of life by making reference to the natural world; here the route is circular, passing through the cycle of the seasons.

> Youth's summer in which we were
>
> I have spent with its autumn:
>
> Winter-age which overwhelms all men,
>
> To me has come its beginning
>
> (Anonymous (Irish), undated)

In contrast, in a third poem, entitled 'Three Score and Ten' and also anonymous, time is referred to as in the passing of days and years, but here the poet only counts the period of active enjoyment:

Our days of age we take no pleasure in;
Our days of grief we wish had never been:
So age deducted, sleep and youth, and sorrow,
Only one span of life is all we borrow

(Anonymous, 1611–51)

All three poems were written in earlier centuries. In modern society, however, we typically describe the journey of life according to the criteria of time. In today's times, time has a plurality of meanings also; we may speak of different temporalities. The concept of time which is most dominant is linear time, in particular clock time and/or chronological time. We may also conceptualise time as it patterns our life course and its constitutent phases. We may speak too about generational time as in the relationship between family generations; and as in historical generations who are separated by their allegiance to different age cohorts and whose lives are shaped by different sets of historical events. Concepts of time as in the March of Time have also been used to suggest human progress (Harvey, 1990; Adam, 1990, 1995; Nowotny, 1994; Kumar, 1995).

Tonight, I propose to explore lives as journeys *in* time and to consider how the experiences of people's lives today are shaped *by* time. I will focus on lives in families and paid work since these have been the settings in which I have done much of my research. I will concentrate on three sorts of time: time as in present time; time as in the life course; and time as framed by historical events and historical period. I want also to engage a little with theory. It is currently fashionable in sociology and other social sciences to place theoretical emphasis upon the ways in which individuals are complicit in constituting and reconstituting their lives. While I would agree with this emphasis, I also want to balance up the picture a bit and bring back into centre stage the old sociological dilemma – the inter-relationship of agency and structure. People are not only agents of their own destinies. Their experiences and actions are constituted with respect to their social locations and the lives of others. These in turn implicate relations of power – within families, organisations, institutions and the wider society. A focus on time may be helpful in this endeavour: the way we constitute our lives processually through time, and the way time through social institutions and structures shapes our lives.

At this juncture and on this type of occasion, a bit of autobiography may be in order. Broadly, my own research can be described as the study of family lives though, at different times, I may have described it differently. Like most sociologists I have studied lives lived in contemporary time. As I look back, I am struck by the particularity of the historical periods in which I undertook the research – which was not at all obvious to me then in the way it is now. I have also become conscious that time has been a central theme in my research. The transition to new life-course phases has been a persistent interest: the study of men and women contemplating separation and divorce, mothers returning to work after childbirth, young people entering adolescence, children starting secondary school, the prospect of grandparenthood. Similarly, I have been interested in the use of time: the distribution of time and labour in marriage and parenthood, the way money and other resources are shared between men and women – too often inequitably – in marriage and in the household. Later, I became interested in the way parents and young people oriented themselves to time. Only recently have I begun to look through the spectacles of history and to understand the importance of historical context in shaping people's lives and perspectives. This latter experience has heightened my consciousness of belonging to the post-war generation and has made me see the dangers of drawing comparisons between younger generations and my own. Each generation seeks to make its own mark on history; the post-1945 generation has done so under unprecedented social and economic conditions quite unlike those of younger and some older generations: the post-1945 establishment of a welfare state, 1960s libertarianism, near full employment until the 1970s, the 1970s women's liberation movement.

Present time

Let me begin with time present. Social scientists typically count the amount of time people spend in the pursuit of different types of activity, for example housework, employment and care. But in our everyday lives, we also speak about deploying time in different ways and not necessarily in relation to chronological time. As workers in the office, we expect and are expected to use time purposefully – 'time is a project'. We work to time schedules. We pack our work into specified units; we think in terms of a working day and working week. As we cross the boundary between work and life outside work, we may draw upon different concepts to describe time. As working mothers and fathers, we may strive to take 'time out'; at weekends and on holiday we depart from the idea of 'time as project' and draw upon notions of 'time as being' – seeking simply to 'spend time' with children, partners, relatives and friends.

Much of the way in which we in Britain talk about our work these days has a time dimension. In the lay language of work as well as in the vocabularies of social scientists words like flexibility, insecurity, and long hours loom large. Increasing reference is made to the term work intensification – the experience of having to work faster and to fit in more and more (Esping-Andersen, Gallie, Hemerijk and Myles, 2002; Brannen and Moss, 1998). Arlie Hochschild (1997) has talked about the existence of a 'time famine' especially among working mothers, who increasingly in this country work not only full time but also hours which exceed the official definition of full-time work.

Under the influence of modern management methods, the way we deploy our time in the workplace is for us to organise and dispense: that is, as long as we meet the targets set for us. Among increasing numbers of professional and technical workers, but also among less skilled workers particularly in the service industry, there is a trend whereby workers are required to dole out their time according to tightly defined time modules. This meting out of time is intended to make us more efficient and productive. Yet this modularisation is undermining normative ideas of what is a 'reasonable amount of time' to spend at work. For the hours we spend working are growing longer; scandalously, the hours of British fathers are still rising (EOC, 2002) and they are working the longest hours in Europe. It is worth stopping for a moment to remember that the idea of a standard day's work, a norm which applied largely to male breadwinners, arose in the context of political struggle about placing *limits* upon the time people spend at work. Recent research from ESRC's Future of Work Programme shows not only a dramatic decline in job satisfaction over the 1990s, it also shows that the greatest drop in satisfaction relates to working hours (Taylor, 2002). Today this dissatisfaction is now more equitably distributed among the workforce, being most marked at the top, among managers and professionals, and, at the bottom, among manual workers (Taylor, 2002). Paradoxically, having more control over organising our time *in* work seems to mean that we are spending longer and longer *at* work.

In today's world, for an increasing number of people, the division between their work and non-work lives is no longer bounded by clear time markers. Those who belong to the flexible workforce, especially those in higher status jobs, increasingly work from and at home, and when they are on the move. All this is made possible by new technology. Modern communications have severed the link between time and space; for example they enable us to ignore country time zones so that we may communicate in real time and work when once we slept. But a downside to these technologies is that email, internet and mobile phone are no respecters of boundaries between home and work. They ignore the natural time rhythms of sleep time and awake time; they can eat into family time, routines, rituals and other commitments. Technology has given us the facility to be forever on call, never off message. It allows us to pack in more and more into our lives. Experientially, time becomes fragmented and speeded up so that tomorrow never seems to arrive (Nowotny, 1994). We live in stretched out time or, as Nowotny has termed it, the 'extended present'. This stretching out of the present is insidious and seductive: because of our fragmented busyness we fail to notice time passing while we work, and we are not unhappy at least at the time – though we may express regret when social scientists ask us questions about it.

Time and space are no longer the arbiters of our public and private selves. Flexibility enables us to connect our work and non-work worlds. Working from home, for example, is family-friendly in enabling us to look after sick children. It is person-friendly when the train system is not functioning. It is worker-friendly in giving us responsibility for managing our time away from the surveillance of management. The flexibility to decide where and when we work, while being a support for employees as well as a benefit to employers, is double-edged. While being an attractive benefit to us individually, it confers enormous responsibility upon each of us to negotiate and also to police the boundaries between work and life outside work. And here is where the concept of the extended present fits in – as I have said, the sense of the future never arriving. For the individual, time present is filled to the brim, never hanging heavy on our hands. Yet a constant state of busyness leaves little time or space to contemplate what lies beyond the present. It not only stops us from imagining the future, it stops us from doing anything about it or making it better. It also has another consequence, I believe; it disconnects us from the *shared* or collective experiences of time, for example rituals and celebrations; for each of us is compelled to create our own time schedules, live in our own time worlds, deciding when to stop work and when to begin again.

Much of the busyness of the modern world of work is to do with multi-tasking; we spend less time on a single focus, and the time it takes us to check the email or reach for the mobile phone gets ever shorter. We make these decisions alone, each of us in charge of managing our own time. Situations which are so individualised leave us in a state of uncertainty about what others may be doing. So we check and recheck the email in the fear of what we may be missing. In this stretched out present we *seem* to act autonomously; at least, we have little sense of being externally controlled. Yet, as research shows, this work intensification manifests itself not only in longer hours but also in the feeling of being under pressure (Burchell *et al.*, 1999; Cully *et al.*, 1999). Such experiences are no longer confined to those on piece rates and assembly lines. Moreover, although most workers report long hours as a requirement of the job, over half admit that they worked long hours because they found the job interesting (Taylor, 2002).

Let me illustrate this ambivalence about work with an empirical example. The case of JJ, as I shall call her, is taken from a study which colleagues and I carried out at Thomas Coram Research Unit and Manchester Metropolitan University; our brief was to examine the impact of the changing world of work upon family life (Brannen, forthcoming). JJ is a mother and a daughter. She is in her late forties and is a call centre supervisor in a bank. During her time in banking, JJ has seen many changes: the disappearance of the old protective paternalism of the bank manager; the demise of 'jobs for life' which in former days were secured in return for employee loyalty; the replacement of the ethic of service with the ethic of sales; the introduction of individual responsibility for staying employable. JJ thought her employer better than most. JJ readily took responsibility for keeping up to date. As she said, these days 'there is so much to know'. She was currently doing a 30-session course in the evenings at the same college as her daughter. Her promotion to supervisor occurred at a particular moment in the call centre's life. The pressure to retain a competitive edge in the globalised world of banking demanded continual cost cutting: whole layers of management had been removed and target times for answering calls at the call centre were constantly being reset, down to 2 minutes per call – worth remembering when next you telephone a call centre!

JJ's daily life, as she describes it, is a constant state of busyness – outside work and inside work. JJ is married to a sales director who is similarly driven by his job. They have two daughters, one of whom is still living at home. As an only child, JJ has responsibility for her frail elderly mother, who lives nearby. JJ's account of her life has many of the qualities of the extended present – a sense of busyness combined with a feeling of autonomy. Yet she often feels that her life is 'out of control'. At the start of her day, JJ describes being already mentally at work as well as attending to domestic matters. At work JJ has to answer calls from the public as well as supervise her team's performance. Such was the pace of the day, she says she often forgets to take breaks, ignores lunchtime, and even puts off going to the loo. Yet, though the pressure leaves JJ little time at work, she still takes charge of collections for colleagues when they retire or leave the bank for other reasons. In taking on this extra work, JJ seeks to observe the time markers that regulated the old bank and to inject the sense of care and community that once typified it. Each night, JJ stays late at work; when she gets home she cooks supper, does some housework and then visits her mother. Most nights she also swats up on work manuals and memos since she has no time to do this at work. These JJ transports home each night in a large box which symbolises the close connection JJ has forged between home and job. Moreover, JJ and her husband are a close couple; each night they spend time talking over their work and care commitments. In effect, JJ's experience of time is subject to a process of intensification both at home and work. Moreover, work and care flow across the boundaries into both settings. In Nowotny's terms, JJ's expectations of time exceed what is realistically possible (Nowotny, 1994).

In this case, the boundaries between work and family life are weakly drawn. Work and care are a compulsion in both contexts. JJ experiences this sense of compulsion as emanating from the *self* rather than from any external source. Significantly, JJ blames *herself* for not managing her time better. Why does she do this? One explanation is that the new management system of the bank depends *less* on visible modes of control, i.e. bureaucratic control, and *more* upon what Basil Bernstein conceptualised as invisible forms of control (Bernstein, 1996). A key medium through which such invisible control is exercised is the language of human resource management and a set of techniques which depend upon communication rather than bureaucratic authority. The new bank offers individuals like JJ a feeling of autonomy on the job – she can decide within limits how to manage her time and how to organise her different work tasks. This autonomy appeals to JJ. It generates a commitment to work which in turn creates a sense of self-actualisation (Rose, 1990). However, the background to this is that the call centre's senior management retains power centrally, chiefly through its control over call-time targets; these targets JJ has to ensure that her team strictly adheres to. While JJ feels fulfilled in her work, she also feels driven. JJ's work practices are infused by the experience of stretched out time. But, in practice, JJ's power in the workplace is rather limited; it resembles the time autonomy she also experiences as a carer and domestic worker and which Ann Oakley identified in her classic study of housework in the 1970s (Oakley, 1974). JJ feels caught up in a present which is crammed 'full to the brim' and where the job is never done. So much so that JJ feels she has no proper 'family time'. Yet, while feeling under pressure, JJ is not a dissatisfied person for JJ feels highly committed both to family and to work, typifying herself as a 'caring person'. Significantly, the work-life and family-friendly policies that the bank advertises and offers its employees play conspicuously little part in enabling JJ to meet her caring responsibilities. Seduced by her busyness, JJ finds it difficult to set her mind to thinking about the future and to taking time off. Moreover, an internalised sense of responsibility for care as well as for her job prevents her from feeling entitled to take advantage of the bank's work-life policies (Lewis, Smithson and das Dores Guerreiro, 2002). And JJ is not alone in this. JJ's ability to envisage a different way of organising work and family life or for moving out of the fast lane is impaired by the process of juggling an individualised, demanding, and multi-faceted present (Daly, 1996). In this context the increasing sense of control over work and the feeling of being increasingly dominated by work is not so paradoxical.

This experience of time represents the lives of those living in 'work-rich', dual-earner households. I could equally well have chosen to focus on the experiences of those whose present time hangs heavily – those with no jobs to go to and fewer resources to enable them fill their time. As Bauman says, those in the 'work world' live *in time*, while space matters little to them. By contrast, those in the workless world live *in space*; in their time 'nothing ever happens' and space dominates time. For if you are poor you must choose cheaper modes of transport; these cost less precisely because saving time and being on time are not guaranteed – at least in theory. The non-employed poor are excluded from the time worlds of the employed: as Pat Allatt has described, the young unemployed stay in bed and lose the impetus to participate in the routines of employed family members (Allatt and Yeandle, 1992). Current public policy in Britain favours the world of work – those with little time to spare – this is the journey we are meant to make.

But even for those in the work world, there is an inherent contradiction between two concepts of time (Daly, 1996). On the one hand, the dual earner lifestyle is driven by Marx's notion of 'time as commodity' with an economic price aimed at the production of profit and efficiency. On the other hand, family life or some aspects of it are construed in relation to notions of morality; in the 'moral economy of time', time ought to be given freely and should not be costed or measured. 'Family time' and 'quality time' are today's symbols of a 'proper' family life. Whether they existed in the past, some historians would argue is a matter for debate (John Gilles (1996), for example). Even so, family time has connotations of process rather than commodity; for social interaction *is* the purpose and outcome of spending time and is not simply a means to an instrumental end. Yet commodity time

– what Daly calls 'a new kind of impatience' (Daly, 1996) – seems to be the time that is winning out.

Not surprisingly, most family-friendly solutions focus upon time and the need to create 'work/life balance'. The term balance suggests an equal time division between paid work and a life outside the job and also a settled accommodation (Taylor, 2001). It seems unlikely that equity and stability can be sustained for very long. For the individual, commitments change over the life course requiring different time frames; moreover, in general family life requires commitment from its members that persists over a *long time frame*. By contrast, for the modern flexible organisation today, the search for financial gain is typically *short-term* and requires commitment from the workforce which is similarly short-term. So, asks Richard Sennett (1998), where are we to find new sources of commitment and trust in a world dominated by the short time horizons of the flexible economy? How can we pursue long-term purposes in a short-term society?

Life-course time

Let me turn now to time as experienced through and in the life course. Shakespeare famously described the seven stages of man – baby, schoolboy, lover, soldier, through to second childhood. Here the idea is that *men* – he doesn't talk about women – follow a single progressive route, although the reference to second childhood conveys a cyclical notion of time. In contrast, the sociological notion of the life course refers to a linear progression of time but not to a single life pathway. Rather, according to Glen Elder (1978), the life course comprises a number of career lines relating to work, parenthood, friendship, sexuality and so on. Like tramlines, career lines may cross over at different points in time and they may proceed in parallel. As agentic beings, we drive our own careers along the tramlines but we do so within a web of relationships with other people and in the context of wider historical, ideological and structural forces. These career lines are punctuated by transitions – moments in time at which we enter and exit from these different career trajectories.

Sociologists typically examine the *timing and sequencing* of life-course phases and transitions. In a study which some of us recently carried out at

Thomas Coram Research Unit, we looked at the patterning of work and care over the life course of three generations (Brannen, Moss and Mooney, forthcoming). We found dramatic changes among mothers in the sequencing and content of the life course; over the generations their employment careers became increasingly more significant and less piecemeal following childbirth. We found changes also in the life course of fathers. Typically men today negotiate several life-course transitions *before* they embark on fatherhood: they complete education and training, they establish themselves in the labour market, they embark on coupledom and home ownership. They stagger these transitions over a relatively long time period, which means that they become fathers at an older age. This elongation of the life course contrasts with the condensed pattern adopted by their own fathers, for whom work, marriage and parenthood happened earlier in the life course and also in much quicker succession.

Attending to the timing and sequencing of the life course has led some sociological theorists to argue that the life course is undergoing destandardisation as part of a general process of individualisation (Beck, 1992, 1994; Beck-Gernsheim, 1996). The structures that once constrained the shape and direction of the life course are said to give way to the power of individuals to construct their own trajectories. Young people, especially, are seen as complicit in the processes of individualisation and destandardisation. As Giddens (1991, 1994) and Beck-Gernsheim (1996) have argued, in lacking external referents, notably of kinship and place, the life course emerges as a 'choice biography' which depends upon the individual's own projects and plans. As Giddens (1991) conceptualises it, individuals construct their trajectories through a process of reflexivity in which the self achieves 'mastery' over social relations and social contexts.

These theories have widespread currency among young people as well as sociologists. However, resources for self-determination and the discourses of the reflexive self are more available to some young people than to others. In a study of young people's orientations to the future, conducted in five European countries, my Norwegian colleague, Ann Nilsen, and I subjected the notion of the choice biography to empirical examination. We found a number of different models (Nilsen and Brannen, 2002; Brannen and Nilsen, 2002). Those whose discourses were closest to the choice biography were young people from relatively affluent backgrounds. These 'can do' young men and women were en route to qualifications via higher education that were likely to provide them with higher status jobs. In contrast, young people who lacked upper secondary schooling and/or were on work training schemes did not view their futures with such a sense of control. But it is important to note that the Norwegian 'choice biographers' who were most likely to think of their futures with expectation – as theirs to plan and to mould – had grown up in a universalist welfare state regime which provided education grants and loans and made them less reliant on their parents for financial support. But these young people did not make reference to the support of public policy.

One lesson, then, that we may draw from this is that is important not only to take account of the decisions and choices that people make but also the non-decisions which make up the backcloth to their lives. For example, as Sarah Irwin suggests (Irwin, 1995), the growth in women's/mothers' employment has brought a significant increase in household income. An unintended consequence of this is that young people today are under less financial pressure to join the labour market at earlier ages. Understanding young people's pathways into adulthood benefits, then, both from a focus upon individual choice but also from a focus upon the structural forces and non-decisions which frame the processual nature of lives lived in time.

Let me take another empirical example. Another life-course transition is the decision to migrate. Although not commonly remarked upon in the daily commentary on migrants in the mass media, such decisions demand enormous courage, enterprise and flexibility on the part of the individuals concerned. Moreover, migrants typically are among the more highly resourced members of the societies they come from, at least in educational terms, and they often bring resources in short supply not only in the originating countries but also often in the host countries they migrate to. Yet we seriously risk underestimating the agency of migrants and the valuable contribution they can make if we fail to understand the forces and contexts which drive people to migrate: forces which operate at many levels and come in many different forms: family pressures, political troubles, economic collapse and decline, personal crises.

The measurement of an individual's progress though the life course is typically made through reference to the concept of age. Rather than withering away, as the theorists of choice biography would have us believe, age remains an extraordinarily powerful concept. Those who study children's lives point to the continuing importance of ideas concerning developmental phases that are considered appropriate for children's ages (Mayall, 1996). These ideas infuse the practices of parents and others who care for children; they have major implications for the way we as adults treat children, the rights we accord them, and the competences we attribute to them. Such ideas can lead us to underestimate children's competences and contributions.

The other end of the life course also seems increasingly, rather than decreasingly, understood in relation to age. Age grading is however a relatively recent trend. Demographers have shown that, over the period 1870–1970, the ages of going to school, entering work and getting married became ever more standardised (Gilles, 1996). This focus on age has, of course, coincided with the unprecedented expansion of the lifetime. Now, it seems, we are more acutely aware of chronological age than ever before. Our consciousness of age quickens as people near points of transition, the notable example being age of retirement, which literally divides an age cohort in two. As John Gilles has argued, earlier generations were much less attuned to such notions of age (Gilles, 1996: 83).

At the same time, with lifestyles becoming healthier and with new medical technologies, cultural conceptions of age are changing. As Martin Kohli (2001) has shown, asked independently of own age, most people say that they feel ten years younger than the age they are. However, such comparisons suggest that people still hold on to stereotypical ideas of age-appropriate looks and behaviour. Indeed, formal retirement age has remained remarkably stable even though we see ourselves as fitter and younger at older ages. Few people go on working beyond 65, and *not* acting our age has done little to reverse this trend. Indeed, in Britain, the trend has been largely in the other direction in recent years – towards ever earlier exits from the labour market (Deven *et al.*, 1998). Moreover, rather than changing cultural perceptions of age, it is the increasing cost of pensions to the public purse which is likely to trigger a rise in retirement age.

Generational time

I turn now to the third concept of time. In discussing present time and life-course time, there is, as I have hinted, another narrative running alongside: historical time and the generations to which individuals belong (Hareven 1982). According to Mannheim (1952) generation units are created especially in the so-called 'formative part' of our lives. The process of becoming a generation unit is twofold: (a) through sharing a similar social location notably relating to social class and (b) through the process of collective exposure to the same historical set of cultural and political events and experiences.

We may examine youth and childhood – two life-course periods much debated today in society – from a generational as well as from a life-course perspective (Alanen, 2001). As those who have studied childhood have suggested, childhood is a cultural invention and a social construction. In effect, what a child experiences and the way we, as adults, construe children and childhood is rarely the same from one era to another. It is important that policymakers and practitioners who make decisions about children's lives – on the basis of assumptions about what children 'need' and what they are capable of – understand this.

Let me give another empirical example. This is taken from the four-generation study I have already mentioned, which examined among other things different generations' conceptions of childhood. The two generations of adults I will refer to were born and brought up in very different historical periods; so the conditions of their childhood were different. The great-grandparent generation was born in the first part of the twentieth century and grew up in the interwar years during the Depression of the 1930s. The grandparent generation was born during or after the Second World War and grew up during post-war reconstruction and the establishment of the welfare state.

Stories about the past are mediated by perceptions of time, as indeed is the writing of history. How people make sense of the past is also shaped by the present and by present life-course phases. I do not propose at this juncture to discuss issues of interpretation. Rather, I want to suggest that generations who share the same historical experiences and social location express through their memories particular discourses of childhood. I want to argue that one way of interpreting these discourses is to view them as *small pockets of history* preserved in individuals (Nielson, 2001).

The oldest generation, the great-grandparent generation, now in their eighties, described their childhoods as part of the general condition of *family life*; they did not identify childhood as a specific phase. Moreover their stories of the past focused on the impact of external events rather than their own agency. They portrayed the structural features of their lives as broad descriptive landscapes. Of course, the interwar years were more homogeneous than the current period in the sense that a much larger proportion of the population worked in manual jobs. There was no welfare state. Especially among working-class people, experience of hard times was common. Working-class members of this generation recalled their childhood as a time of hardship and struggle for the *family*, so that children were often required to give considerable help at home and sometimes to earn money outside the home. This generation also portrayed the past as having fallen heavily on the shoulders of *mothers*; it was mothers who were remembered for keeping families together and enabling the household to 'get by'. Of course, not all working-class members of this generation experienced poverty. But those who escaped poverty remarked on their good fortune while, by contrast, no middle-class members of this generation made reference to the Depression. What is striking here is that even though this generation has witnessed enormous changes in children's lives and in the value accorded to children, none evaluates the past as a loss of childhood.

Some memories are however recast by hindsight. Most members of the great-grandparent generation reflected upon the lack of educational opportunity when they were young. Clearly, both over the last century and over their own life course, this generation has witnessed the growing importance of education for the life chances of subsequent generations, especially for women. Looking back from present vantage points, it was the great-grandmothers who viewed the absence of educational opportunity with most regret.

It is interesting how different are the memories of childhood of the next generation – those born around the last world war. This generation places the *child* at the heart of their remembrances rather than external events. The lives of most people born in the post-war period were indeed materially better and also healthier, notably working-classes lives: families were smaller, there was full employment, there was greater educational opportunity and a developing welfare state (Wadsworth, 1991). The post-war period constituted a break with the past, heralding a new era and new ways of thinking. Ideas about childhood were at the forefront of such change: childhood was seen as a specific life-course phase and as a time *for* children. Yet working-class members of this generation stressed that life was not easy and money was still tight.

Unlike the generation before them, who evaluated their childhood as good or bad, hard or uneventful, this generation assessed childhood in relation to the concept of individual happiness. This generation psychologises childhood: above all else, childhood ought to be a happy time. The material context of childhood and family life shades into the background, while the emotional context comes to the fore. But just as the oldest generation sees mothers as crucial to family's material welfare, so too the next generation considers mothers and mother love to be the key ingredients of a good childhood (and a good adulthood). Unlike the older generation, this 1945 generation makes judgements about their own parents – their mothers especially – and accords them responsibility for childhood. Making reference to the post-war ideology – 'mothers' place is in the home' – they evaluate their mothers according to their efforts to ensure that children did not come home to 'empty houses'. The post-1945 cry 'my mother never left us' is *the* badge of a proper childhood and *the* condition for providing individuals with psychological security. Such a concern contrasts sharply with the older generation's concern with the *household's* material security. The concern with too little space in the home (overcrowding) is replaced in the next generation with the fear of giving children *too·much* space – *emotional space*, that is, when children come home to empty, motherless homes.

Alongside this subjection of childhood to psychology, the 1945 generation recalls childhood as a *collective* experience, not only an individualised one: memories of church outings, the freedom to roam the countryside with their siblings and friends, the pleasures of playing in the street. They also recall family holidays. Family holidays symbolise the advent of the nuclear family ideal. They also reflect changing social conditions: the success of some groups of manual workers in gaining from their employers the right to annual leave and, through the mass production of the motor car, increased geographical mobility (Inglis, 2000). These different concepts of childhood need therefore to be understood historically in the context of changes in social and economic conditions as they differentially affect generations of men and women.

Sociological journeys in time

The title of this lecture promised a sociological journey through time. The lives of sociologists are not exempt from such an examination. In terms of the first type of time I have talked about, typified as the extended present, we researchers too often live out our work lives – brimful of research on the latest policy initiatives – in this way. Moreover, as the markets for research expand, so we marketise our time and mete it out in modules. While there are many positive aspects to this, there are risks also. One cardinal sin is to fail to remember the past and rather too often to reinvent it. Basil Bernstein (2000) warned us of the dangers of the fragmentation of social science knowledge, which occurs when we fail to build upon work created over time. Such fragmentation may lead us to lose our bearings and, rather than breaking down the boundaries between the disciplines, we may build up new walls of silence.

As a sociologist of family life, I am conscious of a shift of interests and perspectives as I, too, move through the life course. Interests shift also as those close to us embark on new transitions, be they the perils of parenthood, the challenges of retirement or the demands of the third age. Sociologists also belong to historical generations. Over time our role has changed but so too have the ideas we draw upon. In the period of my own research career, different theoretical and political concerns have come to the fore, shaping my own generational location and identification, and my research questions. I started in research in the late 1970s, a time infused by the politics of the Women's Movement and a determination to generate greater gender equality and social justice. It is no accident, as they used to say, that Feminist researchers examined the way resources were distributed between men and women. Time, as in 'how much time', was a key measure then of gender equality, both in relation to life-course time and everyday time. The shift in the 1990s from the politics of emancipation to the politics of identity or life politics (Giddens, 1991) has brought different kinds of issues to the fore. This was a period in which voice, difference and identity occupied the theoretical frame, ranging over the terrains of sexuality and childhood as well as gender and race, which, by then, had become firmly established. The study of the construction of subjectivities became increasingly attractive, while sociological questions of power and social justice went underground, particularly as the public politics of neo-liberalism took hold in the 1980s.

The theoretical landscape of the social sciences may be changing again. We may be witnessing a return to an old sociological concern – the dialectic between agency and structure. Moreover, old concepts will return under new guises. One concept which is currently gaining ascendancy in the political arena – it is well established in the social sciences – has special salience to the study of lives and time. This is the concept of care. Care as a concept has particular attractive aspects. Crucially care raises the structure–agency dilemma. On the one hand it suggests the concept of interdependence, that is the way we depend upon one another for care (Finch, 1989; Finch and Mason, 1993; Smart and Neale, 1998; Sevenhuijsen, 1999; Daly and Lewis, 1999; Ungerson, 1997). Care has a transgressive aspect: it makes us think about how, in moral terms, we ought to live our lives in different contexts: how we ought to live our lives in civil society, in families, in workplaces and other settings. Care is centrally about time: how we spend, value and reward time. Sadly, paid care is measured increasingly in terms of one kind of time – time as a commodity. As care is transferred to the market, caring occupations are organised according to the rational economic model – how much time it takes to deliver particular care-giving tasks, while the care of the whole person is lost from view (Waerness, 1999). When paid work is set at such a high premium and care is left to the market, the financial cost of caring has become a central concern. Care and caring are also closely related to life-course time: we give care to others and we need care from others at particular life-course phases, while entry to different caring occupations is often structured by life-course phase – that is, by how paid care work fits in with current family responsibilities. Care raises issues concerning generational time: the reciprocities which take place between family generations, across time and at any one moment in time, and also the pact which exists in civil society between historical generations, as when younger generations provide the pensions of those who have retired, a matter of increasing political concern across Europe.

I am coming to the end of my 'clock time'. In this lecture, I hope I have been able to suggest the relevance of concepts of time to the ways sociologists understand the social world. Today, we experience the speeding up of time – an accelerating pace of change. At the same time, human advancement – the Long March to Progress – has become an outmoded idea. Yet a perspective on time, especially a sense of history, seems ever more urgent. While each generation makes its own mark upon the world, past and present generations remain connected in an historical chain of rights and responsibilities. In being part of the generational chain, we are morally obliged to identify with the suffering and injustices of the past and thereby to engage in processes of reparation and redemption in the present and the future (Cwerner, 2000).

Making the world a better place by finding ways to live together remains a central human quest. Yet this still eludes us; even now across Europe, the embers of fascism are being rekindled. Questioning the belief in Progress should not, as Zigmunt Bauman has argued (1991), mean that we commit 'the sin of post modernity' – that is to 'abandon the effort and to deny the belief'. The quest to live together takes time; democracy takes time; deliberation and negotiation take time. Finding ways to challenge the more insidious forms of power – the non-decisions which never appear on political agenda – takes time and requires an understanding of history, as those of us who have studied the gendered realities of family life know so well. Collectively and individually, we need to consider not only how we can make time, but how we give new value to time. To do this we need to be conscious of how time makes us. I hope this discourse on time has helped to make the point.

References

Adam, B. 1990). *Time and Social Theory*. Cambridge: Polity Press.

Adam, B. (1995) *Timewatch: The social analysis of time*. Cambridge: Polity Press

Alanen, L. (2001) 'Childhood as a generational condition'. In L. Alanen and B. Mayall, *Conceptualising Child-Adult Relations*. London: RoutledgeFalmer.

Allatt, P. and Yeandle, P. (1992) *Youth Unemployment and the Family*. London: Routledge.

Bauman, Z. (1991) 'A sociological theory of postmodernity'. In P. Beilhertz (ed.), *The Bauman Reader*. Oxford: Blackwell.

Bauman Z. (1998) *Work Consumerism and the New Poor*, Buckingham: Open University Press.

Beck, U. (1992) *Risk Society: Towards a new modernity*. London: Sage.

Beck, U. (1994) 'The reinvention of politics: towards a theory of reflexive modernisation'. In U. Beck, A. Giddens and S. Lash (eds), *Reflexive Modernization: Politics, tradition and aesthetics in the modern social order*. Cambridge: Polity Press.

Beck-Gernsheim, E. (1996) 'Life as a planning project'. In S. Lash, B. Szerszynski and B. Wynne (eds), *Risk, Environment and Modernity: Towards a new ecology*. London: Sage.

Bernstein, B. (1996) *Pedagogy, Symbolic Control and Identity: Theory, research, critique*. London: Taylor and Francis.

Bernstein, B. (2000) *Pedagogy, Symbolic Control and Identity: Theory, Research, Critique*. Lanham, MD: Rowman and Littlefield.

Brannen, J. and Moss, P. (1998) 'The polarization and intensification of parental employment in Britain: consequences for children, families and the community'. *Community, Work and Family*, 1, 3: 229–47.

Brannen, J. and Nilsen, A. (2002) 'Young people's time perspectives: from youth to adulthood'. *Sociology*, 36, 3: 513–37.

Brannen, J., Moss, P. and Mooney, A. (forthcoming) *The Changing Work/Life Balance: Generations of working and caring*.

Brannen, J. (forthcoming) 'Time, work and care in a changing world: the case of a woman bank worker'. In A. Leira and T. Boje (eds), *Welfare policy and family: gender work and care.*

Burchell, B., Day, D., Hudson, M., Lapido, D., Mankelow, R., Nolan, J., Reed, H., Wichert, C. and Wilkinson, F. (1999) *Job Insecurity and Work Intensification.* York: Joseph Rowntree Foundation.

Cully, M., Woodland, S., O'Reilly, J. and Dix, G. (1999) *Britain at Work: As depicted by the 1998 Workplace Employee Relations Survey.* London: Routledge.

Cwerner, S. (2000) 'Research note: the chronopolitan ideal: time, belonging and globalisation'. *Time and Society*, 9, 2/3: 331–45.

Daly, K. (1996) *Families and Time: keeping pace in a hurried culture.* London: Sage.

Daly, M. and Lewis, J. (1999) 'Introduction: conceptualising social care in the context of welfare state restructuring'. In J. Lewis (ed.), *Gender, Social Care and State Restructuring in Europe.* Aldershot: Ashgate.

Deven, F., Inglis, S., Moss, P., Petrie, P. (1998) *A State of the Art Review on the Reconciliation of Work and Family Life for Men and Women and the Quality of Care Services.* Norwich: Her Majesty's Stationery Office.

Elder, G. (1978) 'Family history and the life course'. In T. K. Hareven (ed.), *Transitions: The family and the life course in historical perspective.* New York: Academic Press.

EOC (2002) Press release. London: Equal Opportunities Commission.

Esping-Andersen, G., Gallie, D., Hemerijk, A. and Myles, J. (2002) *A new welfare architecture for Europe?* Report submitted to the Belgian Presidency of the European Union. Brussels: European Union.

Finch, J. (1989) *Family Obligations.* Cambridge: Polity Press.

Finch, J. and Mason, J. (1993) *Negotiating Family Responsibilities.* London: Routledge.

Giddens, A. (1991) Modernity and Self-Identity: *Self and society in the late modern age.* Cambridge: Polity Press.

Giddens, A. (1994) 'Living in a post-traditional society'. In U. Beck, A. Giddens and S. Lash, *Reflexive Modernization: Politics, tradition and aesthetics in the modern social order.* Cambridge: Polity Press.

Gilles, J. (1996) *A World of their own Making: Myth, ritual and the quest for family values*. Cambridge, MA: Harvard University Press.

Hareven, T. K. (1982) *Family Time and Industrial Time: The relationship between family and work in a New England industrial community*. Cambridge: Cambridge University Press.

Harvey, D. (1990) *The Condition of Postmodernity*. Cambridge: Blackwell.

Hochschild, A. (1997) *The Time Bind: When work becomes home and home becomes work*. New York: Metropolitan Books, Henry Holt and Company.

Inglis, F. (2000) *The Delicious History of the Holiday*. London: Routledge.

Irwin, S. (1995) 'Social reproduction and change in the transition from youth to adulthood'. *Sociology*, 29, 2: 293–317.

Kohli, M. (2001) 'Dividing the life course: are chronological age boundaries an anachronism?' Paper given at the European Sociological Association conference, Helsinki, August.

Kumar, K. (1995) *From Post-Industrial to Post-Modern Society. New theories of the contemporary world*. Oxford: Blackwell.

Lewis, S., Smithson, J. and das Dores Guerreiro, M. (2002) 'Young people's sense of entitlement to support for the reconciliation of employment and family life'. In J. Brannen, A. Nilsen, S. Lewis and J. Smithson (eds) (2002) *Young Europeans, Work and Family Life: Futures in transition*. London: Routledge.

Mannheim, K. (1952) *Essays on the Sociology of Knowledge*. London: Routledge and Kegan Paul.

Mayall, B. (1996) *Children, Health and the Social Order*. Buckingham: Open University Press.

Nielson, H. (2001) 'Historical, cultural and emotional meanings: interviews with girls in three generations'. Paper given at the Center for Working Families, University of California Berkeley, 19 March. Centre for Women's and Gender Studies, University of Oslo.

Nilsen, A. and Brannen, J. (2002) 'Theorising the individual – structure dynamic'. In J. Brannen, A. Nilsen, S. Lewis and J. Smithson (eds), *Young Europeans, Work and Family Life: Futures in transition*. London: Routledge.

Nowotny, H. (1994) *Time: The modern and postmodern experience.* Cambridge: Polity Press.

Oakley, A. (1974) *The Sociology of Housework.* London: Martin Robertson.

Rose, N. (1990) *Governing the Soul: The shaping of the private self.* London: Routledge.

Sennet, R. (1998) *The Corrosion of Character: The personal consequences of work in the new capitalism.* New York: W. W. Norton.

Sevenhuijsen, S. (1999) *Citizenship and the Ethics of Care: Feminist considerations on justice, morality and politics.* London: Routledge.

Smart, C. and Neale, B. (1998) *Family Fragments.* Cambridge: Polity Press.

Taylor, R. (2001) 'The future of work-life balance', *An ESRC Future of Work Programme Seminar Series.* Swindon: ESRC.

Taylor, R. (2002) 'Britain's world of work – myths and realities', *An ESRC Future of Work Programme Seminar Series.* Swindon: ESRC.

Ungerson, C. (1997) 'Social politics and the commodification of care'. *Social Politics*, 4: 362–81.

Wadsworth, M. E. J. (1991) *The Imprint of Time.* Oxford: Oxford University Press.

Waerness, K. (1999) 'The changing "welfare mix" in childcare and care for the frail elderly in Norway'. In J. Lewis (ed.), *Gender, Social Care and State Restructuring in Europe.* Aldershot: Ashgate.